THE POEMS OF EXPERIENCE

ZORA CEKO

MINERVA PRESS
WASHINGTON LONDON MONTREUX

THE POEMS OF EXPERIENCE

ISBN 1 85863 753 8

First Published 1996 by
MINERVA PRESS
195 Knightsbridge
London SW7 1RE

Printed in Great Britain by
B.W.D. Ltd., Northolt, Middlesex

THE POEMS OF EXPERIENCE

ABOUT THE AUTHOR

Zora Ceko was born on 10th August 1926 in Šibenik, in the Dalmatia region of Croatia. She read Agricultural Science at the University of Zagreb and graduated in 1952.
During the Second World War, Ceko and her family were engaged in the People's Liberation Movement under Tito and having lost three family members in the fighting, she was later forced to seek refuge in Australia. She gained Australian citizenship, and between 1956 and 1965 worked at the Agricultural Department of Victoria, in Melbourne.
Returning to her native Croatia, Ceko was employed in the tourist industry; the new and dynamic branch of the Yugoslav economy. She retired in 1991 just before the outbreak of war and the dissolution of the former Yugoslavia.
Although currently working on an English sequel to *The Poems Of Experience,* the author plans to have her poetry published in Croatian as soon as the political situation allows: *"This bloody war hangs over our heads like a boulder. It is as cruel as it is long. The Croats have known years of peril and catastrophe but we shall endure, for sure...* "
Zora Ceko is unmarried and still lives in Šibenik.

THE POEMS OF EXPERIENCE were written in shelter during the siege of Šibenik, Croatia, from 16th September 1991 till 10th August 1993.

Dedicated to The United Nations

1

"Forget me not" sing the flowers on its colour-flute:
I am the colour of soul imbued in peacock's tail.
Look how it shades the light down its feather smooth
With riot of shimmer dazzling as house of snail.

O, what shall I do when I am what I behold?
Rejoicing of fear and trembling of happy end.
I hear a hammer on life's auction and voice: "It's sold!"
In spite of Holy Grail kept in other broker's hand.

And the light plays colour – flute to get us blind.
And we thirstily drink the sound from its deep.
In spherical womb of light dreams our Earth kind
and doubts whether to awaken us before hibernal sleep.

2

We sing: "Mater Dei ..." bowing the head.
We carry the Cross and God on it.
Yet we call another to come and give us bread
and holy Ghost to dwell by our hearth lit.

When we meet a worthy "Mater" we dishonour her,
contaminate her path, womb and cheers –
she may not bring forth a desirous Sir,
lest we suffer further for two thousand years.

And we are the torch turned toward dark space,
dark as a fearful night, dark as a grave,
dark as a love that we in vain race,
run after it like a lord, hero or a slave.

3

Glory to you O daybreak, sunrise,
dawn of life, heart of sure awake!
Forward, rush on, rather than otherwise,
Eternal rebirth has plenty to give and take.

I know that I am here, now and yonder,
gazing at flow of matter that doesn't matter,
that swings, twists, rushes and wander
far away between the fire and deep ether.

Hold on! Let daybreak last for awhile,
till we find our way out of dark night.
We don't want to stay forever in exile,
O dawn of life, glad glow, O happy sight!

4

We are not the same. We are far away:
from our source we reached the mighty flow.
Now we have nowhere to stop, to sway,
to return, to cry for help, to say "No!"

There is nothing the same any more.
We stand alone face to face with deadly threat.
The force of universe draws us to its core
and now we must follow even in regret.

We cannot crawl behind the nature's wit,
The beasts are at bay, scarce and meek.
We ought to run, to fly, to dash a bit
to reach the ORDER although young and weak.

5

Where are you going, my brother?
You are equipped as in Trojan War.
I cry for you, I tremble, I shudder -
I don't want you to die like a boar.

You aim at them and they aim at you,
By all means they shoot and you do alike.
The all means are invented and more are through,
You are prepared to be struck if you miss to strike.

The more we grow in number and more we spread
like wheat or barley over fertile land
the more we are suppressed - alive or dead,
exposed to wind of changes and scattered like sand.

6

"Where are you?" I call from mountain alone.
"Here I am, can't you see?" answered the sound.
And I look and hear only: din-don, din-don
coming from infinity rebounding of ground.

O heavenly present, gift of thirsty mind!
You hear what you wish, see what you stride.
But nothing is there for deaf and blind.
The strange mocking stars don't abide.

We are many like fish astounded and mute
moving through mist ahead, left and right,
gather together, follow enchanting lute
unable to break the bonds that keep us tight.

7

I saw her light and slender, unleavened like bread,
wrinkled stooped alone along the road.
She looked at me as to say: "Why am I so sad?"
I wished to relieve her and take over her load.

I wished to answer her beseeching crude
that plead accuse and damn without pardon.
In time of peril, the pity sounds rude,
bruises and aches although in divine garden.

She stood old, puzzled, gazing at me.
The whole planet appeared as an apple ripe
tossed from age to age far from holy tree
weeping day and night unable tears to wipe.

8

O bell-tower, for what are you tolling so?!
You witness us calling out the dark space to sing.
You redeem us, lead us steady, although slow,
to Elysian fields forever to toll and ring.

Echo your sounds far and wide, advance “Panta rhei”
endlessly tolling, monotonous yet as a prayer in need.
We ensure a pious train, move on in fear and dismay
like bare-footed pilgrims that walk and bleed.

O bell-towers, who ever hung the bells at you
to stand aloft and toll when we care and strive?!
You are our messengers, only one amongst few.
You sound our pain as to herald that we are alive.

9

Look man what you did and ever do the same?
Willy-nilly you do. O, you ... you bloody lot!
Repeat your bloody ordeal without remorse or shame,
for you appear slow to solve and quick to plot.

You lie, you forge, you are a false brute
that shades the blood like water over spring;
whether of beast, man or woman, child or angel mute.
You run the call of blood like a thirsty sting.

Never tired, never "stop it," never "no, no!"
You are fellow of darkness chained to hard rocks
that consumes your liver and causes again to grow
that doesn't kill but afflicts, disdains and mocks.

10

What for, did I dip in thoughts and did I sigh,
watched the stars and called God alone?
Nobody ever waited for me or bid me goodbye;
They stood like thorns against me saying "be gone."

And I went from one corner to uncertain end,
across the land, oceans and many seas.
As a Sphinx that surveys the world and its trend
I gazed in wonder and from joy fell upon my knees.

It seemed to me that I saw "Eureca's" door;
not leading to mount Ararat for eternal fire,
nor to Southern Cross for inexhaustible golden ore,
but to new realm beyond history and its empire.

11

Ages passed by like shadow behind the moon.
People swelled and moved where they could,
Up and down like ants when a storm is about soon.
Their sprouts spread like grass to every blessed mood.

And the people are like grass that keeps together to stand:
Together they grow, fight, travel, cling to and dance;
They stick to company, collect like water or sand.
As corn on wind they swing, as disease they advance.

People look “out” and “in” repeat and do the same.
“Out” – to pull, to push, to squash, to grab, to take.
“In” – to regret, to expiate, to punish, to blame.
They are still by naval tied unable to force the break.

12

The waves of ocean rush on to hard shore
creating bays, gulfs, straits, sounds, coves.
The water must roll on and on, dash and bore
like wine in wood that old horse faraway tows.

So the waves of flesh roll from East to West
after the sun, like sunflowers or a flying flock.
They move to rise up like a wave to its crest
and fall back in a roar, foam and continue to rock.

Likewise Slav people moved from East to West
from one ocean to the other always in tidal rush.
Never to gain shelter but as a bird in its nest
shivering from fear, yet ready, fearless charge
and crush.

13

The Slavs crossed the land over mountains and plains,
like a river in spate they filled empty space to dwell.
They cleared the ground,
grew through its pores and veins
and suffer alone for others like sand in a pearl shell.

And as sheep that graze, venturing far ahead,
encounter wolves and tremble deadly scared,
So they stood exposed to lose their very life and stead
and be devoured whenever the beasts dared.

They were tossed like leaves torn off the tree.
Sometimes far away, sometimes in a proper yard.
They used to withstand, struggle, sudden to flee.
They are confined along the frontier, never at rest,
always on guard.

14

Hello there! Who is coming?
Forward my friend, if you are.
The door is open day and night.
Don't rush, nor hesitate.
The time is waiting outside,
Keeping watch to switch the light.

We are here the day of today.
We look, live and hope
in our day bright and clever.
Whose "the day" will be tomorrow?
Will it be a salvation's scope
or will it retard from us for ever?

15

O, how light is the heaven!
Numberless stars keep the watch.
I sit and hold it on my head.
I cherish it, talk to and kiss it.
I bear it on my palm as a feather
with holy sense as from salt and bread.

O, how light is the heaven!
It draws my heart higher and higher,
easy ... easy! So easy is to rise!
It's much harder to stand up
on native ground though uprooted
in spite of its wisdom and its size.

16

Dark ages are always at the door.
O, man how could you exist?
Like germs that kill now as before
and no flash can stop it or resist.

Dark ages come on time's wing –
Birds of universe appear to be gone.
They touch me and you, and everything
and shine in mist waiting for dawn.

17

You will get the age of old days
when your wishes will become short and dizzy,
when you'll walk astray – no ways
to turn here and there light and busy.

To kill, to postpone, to destroy – walk behind,
as the shadow walks behind the wounded bear.
And the tender soul will stray looking for mind
calling in cry to heaven here and there.

18

Hard like ages is the human law:
Doesn't match the nature and its code;
Runs and hides in dark ground below;
Appears like rain and disappears far abroad.

Yet, no authority is left for right thought.
The beast is at ease wherever its lair.
O, brothers, what we've done and brought
to our home unable offspring to spare!

19

Now I am going to write a wise song,
unusual being the words in rhyme
as it is everything sudden but long
in waiting for just or casual time.

A song of people, of divine being
that walks proudly towards the end.
Is there anything so striving
for goodness spreading evil at hand?

Is there anything like a divine soul
that dreams of God and prays for right,
doing wrong as if it would be the only goal –
To kill, to destroy, to extinguish living light?

20

Why are they telling us the lie?
Always the same through depth of race.
Pushing us to kneel, to pray, to die
for good Father – master of the space.

There nothing was nor cannot appear
without one prepared to give
trembling of desire in haste and fear
and the other craving to trace it and receive.

When the third of two bursts into life
it must dispose resources to exist.
Existence is born of need to strive,
pressed by the urge to withstand and resist.

21

I am, you are, born to create,
to think, to search, to deal.
We know the numbers to calculate.
We possess the means to cure and kill.

The nature has given us God and Faith.
But we want them not although we swear.
We are born in suspicion and hate
Weaving the iron shirt in distress to wear.

22

Behold! Around the wonders unnoticed before –
If you had, you would be happy and calm,
Instead, you are desperately bored
leaning the precious head on hard palm.

Behold! We are in the garden of paradise,
here and now. We eat apples when we get,
and if we want. There is nothing we despise
except ourselves, as if for a bet.

We praise our Creator and His creation
for everything He gave us wrapped in thorns.
For we are sick of prayer and humiliation,
sorry of being so invented as sack of horns.

23

"Alle Menschen werden Brüder" - hail, hail!
O brothers sing your hymn all and thus
Let our little globe glare of trustworthy bail,
Let it spin around in glory for being mother of us.

"Alle Menschen werden Brüder" - for ever.
Let those born live in joy and happy lore.
Like birds that gather and flock, their endeavour
to fly to a better world where they each other adore.

"Alle Menschen werden Brüder" - as they are:
Hand to hand, mind to mind, view to view.
We are the flower seasoned by our staggering star
bound to flourish thence in cradle of living dew.

24

From Adam till day of today
We await our Saviour to cure our soul.
We are certain in his coming if we pray
and praying wait, and on and on dole.

The prophets ordained our penitence to endure
time and ages and mutation of our scope.
Through each trying stage we ought to mature
and reach the gate of ever hidden hope.

Alone we must cross the stream of “be or not”,
Convey across the ocean our living urge,
forsake illusive promise that we ever got,
and evade afflictions that on us fiercely surge.

25

O God! How could they crucify Thy son with a thief?
Accuse Him and banish behind the time
and leave us alone like seals on bare reef
to groan, to bite and breed immersed in crime?

How can we call Thee any more praying to hear,
for murmur of our words sickens the air and ground?
And now we crawl after Thee.
I beseech you to come near!
Like a baby lost in a wood we howl and ramble around.

We search and search to step on Thy way,
but we only circle like planets around the sun.
Wherever we turn, nowhere is Thy sacred ray.
We are driven to a Beginning which we shun.

26

The soil composed of stellar dust
cradles the seeds of light and water.
It transmits love to barren lust
full of violence, betrayal and slaughter.

But there are fields that alight rainbows,
and ragged slopes gardened by the sweat
of Croatian people which through ages glows,
spreading a message of love lest we forget.

They cried out to endure for a thousand years.
They gathered soil to cover the roots of human tree
and built the stony gardens shading the tears,
watering spirit of land that genius sets free.

27

There are silly chickens with little brains
cackling all day about eggs and cocks.
From above lightning's blaze, there drops rain.
The senseless power rolls billets and rocks.

... never to cure nature's angry trait
And human efforts pass by in vain.
Then shaker of Earth refuses to wait
the hope of victory bidding "all over again".

28

We are sailing toward the end.
There is nothing that may stop us.
The Beginning is behind the bend.
We cannot sail by heart in hope to pass.

Run man, run day and night!
Look inside, don't mind around.
Forget mother and father, wrong and right.
Where we didn't want to go, now we are bound.

For we long waited suffering in pain.
Long we tried intellect to affirm and seize,
reason to repossess, clear sense to gain,
the best of our notions exert to prize.

29

Come now brothers, the time gets cold,
We've reached the gate of no return.
Come now, forward, young and old,
Kneel and kiss the ash before we burn.

Why... we are crooked, poor and sour.
Our mind wriggles like a snake through wheat.
We look high, seeing low, without power
to repair our sight and devise heart beat.

Do come now! See what we've done
by telling lies, fighting for land and creed.
There is no time to reach shelter by running
nor to stand by, to hop like frogs in thick reed.

30

Fire is condensed in wood and stone,
drawn off the sun from the birth
of our glade where we dwell alone,
unaware of duty toward the mother Earth.

And fire we create to despise the sun,
to burn what is cooled in haste and hate.
We don't know what we've yet done
nor what we'll do till it appears late.

Fire we eat and fire eats us too.
By slow decree we continue to grow lame.
Then the red wigged lord is due
to take us forever from where we came.

31

Wherever I turn, wherever I look
I see armour, shiny guns ready to roar
as if I would be a fish stuck on hook
or a worm wriggling under the pace of war.

And the language doesn't mean to speak.
And the songs are not sung but for a din.
I see the people bent, sick, hungry, weak
ready for seduction to worst of sin.

Violence is Bible immersed in breath of age.
The motion and aspiration stand far apart.
We are frightened, astounded as a bird in cage,
drunk on despair although sober and smart.

32

Be firm my son!
Be steady and wise my son.
Don't rush nor hesitate.
You never know what is behind the hill,
What is behind the wall.
Keep alert your mind
but be calm and not still.

Be great!
Whatever is your size
Be great my son
Whatever you do or have done.

33

"Sic transit gloria mundi," has been said
in the time of wise Romans who were cruel and cheats.
So, the glory passed away as a mistress over paid,
never to return and look in hole of her royal seats.

But, what is "Glory" and where does she now glare
leaving us behind after battle and row?
From where did she come and what does she there?
O mighty one with bitter fruits on eternal bough.

How many troubles did you cause to our world?
For every head yearns to garland neck with you,
although that which passed remains as gold
shining alone in dark treasury without value.

34

The ants march always in a hurry lined up after each
other
like sturdy soldiers that must obey, walk and walk.
They turn back again and again as a baby to its mother,
for the common cause has wrought their doom'd yoke.

Under common law all beings carry an allotted burden
as a chained bear that dances although weary and sad.
We also march in line through roses in a thorny garden,
We hesitate and rebel sometimes for being unjustly led.

We smite and curse our only but deceitful star
that lent us arrows and lured us to open a horror gate.
Set us on the loose sardonic throne saying:
"Ave my Czar."
And now we march like ants trying to master the fate.

35

What delights you O human race, bound to past?
In the course of time we've trained sense of price.
We've built walls, towers, palaces, monuments to last,
then we paint it, sell and forge to bargain with it twice.

We graze sheep on grassy slopes or meadows blue,
gaze at wind-mill or sit with a running creek beside,
then we paint it, take it home and admire as being true
adulterating thus our cosmic path by artificial pride.

We behold pyramids as the portrait of the living mind
and want that to last which blossomed in lasting eve.
We forget and search, forget and look to find
what is hidden, getting always less than we give.

36

When wind blows it has the way to pass.
Blows in directions unmarked on the elusive sky.
So the ghost of the world precipitates from living glass
without a sign or mark and inexhaustible cannot dry.

And then appears the question of galling lot.
Who takes more, who less, who'll crawl, who'll fly.
The wings of evil tear forth as sudden blast - shot
blowing like wind over canes that whistle and sigh.

Everything settles somehow after damage is done.
Revenge is a human way paved by an eternal cry.
A revenge daughter of evil, generates the law of the gun,
dwells in shadow of conscience,
echoes and asks no "Why!"

37

Knowledge comes by way of desire and chance
like a bird on its wings nesting in joyous spring.
It comes and goes leaving behind a magic lens
to magnify the memory sealed in its genetic ring.

We found signs of procedure that count
every seed and every ray that glows in organic shine.
We carry our vow up and down the sacred mount
looking through experience for a last almighty sign.

And comes the hour when knowledge turns back
like water running over a precipice down and down.
So, the candles emit light and then gradually slack,
extinguish in futility, like the laughter of a clown.

38

The people follow its duty and, bent forward, march
after the call from outerspace, unknown and very far.
Duty bids them “bye”
and leaves their last breath to lurch,
surrendering body to dust and soul to coveted star.

The paths are always crowded and the pass broad.
There we all serried march in horror though yet obliged.
It seems no end of that endless painful road
where we resemble a silent army,
in a useless battle, engaged.

And the people continue always in the same manner.
Again and again they gush and swarm to a common goal.
Justice with bloody crown leads the way
and carries a banner
and draws the train nearer to the chasm of cosmic hole.

39

The living world in world seen and beyond, unseen
has devised the senses to sense the manner of long fare,
ready to lose, to run hazard in order once to win.
O, feelers of universe, brave envoys that know and dare!

You sense to beware us, lead us as a skilful bard.
You dress us to resist the pressure of turbid clouds.
As a housekeeper that, keeping watch,
keeps locked his yard and for no risk walks about,
cheers himself and often shouts.

Senses stand as our web stretched across firmament,
and like a spider which collects
the living matter in fright,
drinks it with heavenly dew for short merriment
knowing that senses sense the downfall of wrong and
right.

40

As a thorn in the heel of the bare-footed
forced to walk away
who cannot stop to pull it out and free the run.
So is my heart apt to bleed and sorrowfully ache, today,
nagging my conscience as if I should be the only one.

Where shall I go, where shall I turn in the dark?
The light leads me, but there is no light elsewhere.
O, blessed be a dog that, lost in blizzard, stops to bark,
howls now and then, licking paws that to frost adhere.

Dog'll find the way tracing its bloody chart,
But shall we ever reach the end of this torrid lent?
Like a thorn in walking heel stands the pain in my heart,
and aches as suffering of people under
"Balance of Power" bent.

41

“Stop the war in Croatia” - harken Ye deaf and slow!
Stop the war! Stop the war if you are what you
reckoned!
They wage war for land and sea, pushing us in cold
shadow
to dream about awakening and never ever to be
awakened.

“Stop the war in Croatia!”
Ye that have induced our martyrdom,
Killed our houses, burned our spirits to blot us out at last.
Come now out of your infernal nest, your secular
boredom
to broad meadows where our graves speak the truth
of the past.

Stop the war Ye warriors of unapproachable age!
It’s long way to come, yet short to cross the sacred
bridge
to the other side.
As the book that starts its story from the last page,
so you do, slaves of hate, cast off for ever
to stand the siege.

42

O, how broad is our marvellous globe,
Holy TERRA – the mother!
The beauty among planets,
these Olympic runners of universe.
As many as stars in heaven are
the beings born from each other,
irrationally-shaped, embroidered,
tinged to be better dispersed.

So is the land which bore plants
and beasts mirroring its worth
in sky, mountains,
lakes and lucid waters in rush,
where people grow like mushrooms
hasten back and forth
and incited by temporal urge
often collide and crush.

There are many countries on our TERRA –
Mother, the globe,
but only one is BOSNIA,
beautiful maiden in native array.
Only one is BOSNIA standing like truth –
pillar on probe and tears its heart
calling for help from U.N. crossway.

43

It's late in the night, night without lights,
deep night, thick and heavy, thorough black.
The heavy guns belch and belch. Nothing so bites -
as fear, as sleepless awakening till bellow slack.

The arms coldly belch at me and my mind.
I cannot endure, though to escape I don't dare.
I have to stay and listen to its thundering ride,
I must wait and tremble as a hunted hare.

The whole night the rocket launchers sing,
and howl in orgy, full of blood and fear.
I have to listen to the horror symphony
in its middle ring,
and wait till murderers change its gear.

44

As a barrel that churns on a cart full of “White horse”,
a long way over a rough road, and, losing its bung,
spills it out and flattens and no remorse
can restore anew its spirit forever slung.

The same is true of the spirit of human mind lost in time,
carried through events full of danger and pain.
No songs can return to its exalted rhyme
nor wisdom to its well filled with baleful rain.

It’s a trying era for human seeds on Earth,
for every ferocious bird craves to grab it and loot.
Between the hell and sunshine we sail to berth
the vessel of our torment and at dawn try another route.

45

O, my little son, smile I beg.
You are born to smile again.
War has cut your little leg.
Your little thigh hangs in vain.

O my little child, my son,
You'll never wear a pair of shoes,
never after a rainbow run.
But don't ever your smile lose.

46

On Balcan where dogs dance with wolves around fire
is not easy to guard the flock and walk about.
Horizon is shut by mountains where lonely friar
waits for evening bells that at human misdeed shout.

Women as squirrels peer out from their uneasy abode
not knowing what'll bring tomorrow with daybreak.
Ought they miscarry or will the hope its burden unload?
What to do with hoyden daughters and fair sons at stake.

On Balcan quaint roses grow in abundance to wither
quick.
As a falcon struck by lightning falls down from a height
and, bleeding to death, eyes the sky to slack his wick,
so Balkans die thirsty of life wrenched by voracious
blight.

47

They walk through rain and snow under the gun-shells,
old and little side by side, bundled babies. Tear after sigh!
They walk, turn around, listen.
"Ave Maria" - toll the knells.
Refugees hurry in dismay through wind far from God's eye.

They keep walking to flee, retreating
like army not knowing "where".
Cold with icy teeth bites their eyes and pale cheeks.
They have nothing to eat
except lean wolves or lagging bear.
They have nowhere to arrive except to flee days and weeks.

And they flee crouched through rain
and wind over their native land.
They cry and tear to open snow - drifts for bit of rest.
They walk crucified under heavy grenades as in legend:
Be sacrificed old and little and babies on mothers' breast.

48

Be well, sleep better,
brave new world of perjured behaviour!
Turn to the other side before you awake,
for awake life may spare.
The time has passed forever beyond the era of
"No" Saviour.
"No" better and "No" the worst.
O grievous spirits lazy to stir.

As a shepherd that busies himself
mowing clover for hay,
leaves his flock on the mountain,
for a while free to graze,
which soon becomes scented
and shattered by beast of prey
and thus all his hard gains irreparably
vanish as in blaze.

So we do. Build schools to teach,
hospitals to cure the sick,
bridges to span the chasms,
tame rivers to convey our trades,
rise over the sky to near the stars
to travel safer and quick.
Then all of a sudden pull it down,
destroy to nil in savage raids.

Awake now or never my brothers
with backward view!
Don't sleep enchanted by false hope
under a soft pillow.
Look at trees along the flowing water
standing in queue,
with its joyful crowns always smiling as weeping willow.

49

I wonder how old is a mountain range,
that lies in front of my desire!
Is it sister of strange Stonehenge
or a daughter of ash and fire?

I ask, how old is the stone under?
Does it mutate only in rage?
Are we also like mountains I wonder –
out of time, without the age.

50

I hear shelling, shooting explosions and painful screams.
War is before my gate as "Hannibal" of Roman reign.
O, where is now my cave which I often perceive in dreams
where I could hide and kindle fire and sit far from human stain?

And war resembles the device of a distorted mind - sick affair,
when people are persuaded to wage it against other people,
command life or death,
convert mental ardour into nightmare,
victimise survivors not to recover
but stay unsound and crippled.

They sacrifice fortune to obtain means
for such a ghastly show.
Affliction bursts forth like an earthquake,
afflicting all.
O, where is my cave now,
that I may sit with reverent bow
before the fire -
queen of Begging and End on Grand ball?

51

We are like the leaves on a tree –
crown that cannot roots replace,
but stay upward as envoys of the land
to the realm of royal sun,
forbidden to turn back
but only forth looking at the face
of Supreme Judge till he hammers:
"All right, it's done."

And leaves keep together to stand draught and wind
and guard its tree from all kinds of nature's wit.
So are the people that travel far
to reach the sacred river Ind,
to wash their bodies in the past for a future
in a world confused and split.

We are also as leaves on the tree
of the human illusive drive,
grown through a mist of duration
not aware of its end.
The purport we'll never solve
no matter how long we strive
being like the leaves that function
under sunshine on dark land.

52

Now you are turning the pages of a book,
and inexperience read
and learn about happenings,
why and how it came to pass.
You see, at first they kill
because someone something needs,
causing havoc,
breaking all ties in fury as bold as brass.

Then the writers for centuries write about events thence
which have been so well staged
in theatres of common disaster:
there keeps vigil a sacred bond
between evil and penitence
and we don't know its origin
nor its assiduous master.

And now it seems that we have turned the last page.
The book is closed with title that radiates –
"BEWARE!"
We ought to rise like morning sun or evening star
and potent sage in new bond of human survival –
sanctuary of new welfare.

53

Experience is apple inherited from Adam and Eve,
that grew in paradise during the time of temptation.
It kept dark the knowledge training us to grieve
till we seized it, paying in blood of each generation.

The payment never helped to settle a forged bill,
and experience has to be planted over and over again.
Always "ab ovo," drill after a futile drill.
Tribute in blood lured the land to yield us grain.

Thus we came on Cross to point of no return,
Although we continue to move with apple
as loud genetic bell,
From experience we did not abhor nor even learn.
There is no other way than to swallow
our tempting apple and say farewell.

54

A dear youth passed by and waved me to wait.
O how he was happy; smiling,
he kissed me, telling his story.
Machine-gun, bombs and various insignia
on him were great
as he himself was being a warrior,
fighter, God of victory.

From that time I saw him no more
and my heart was torn.
I was told that he bravely served
and consequently fell in battle.
Whenever I passed there,
I wait and depressed silent mourn
like reeds on winds that totter
and sob unable to settle.

And now I remember him as a baby,
how he cried, squalling bitter,
never surrendering to mother's caresses,
protesting at being born.
When we last met he radiated
as a flower prepared soon to wither.
He felt, knew it, refusing to vegetate
as a convert of a world forlorn.

55

Poems are like prayer at one's leisure in evening's late,
that takes rise from emotion deep tightened by urgent love,
inflexible, strong as accomplished will, as pursuit of fate,
as message of spiritual age, brought by the white innocent dove.

Poems are exalted, a love of the inexhaustible living ghost
spread from one to the other being by prolific cosmic rays
that pulsate in pulses of broods and wings
that rise and boast
and never subside but swell.
Heart of universe loves and prays.

But love dreams in poetry, erupts in rapture of souls within
excited by duty to obey course of Order beyond presence.
Nobody knows how it performs,
where abides when hasn't been
nor its vigour that generates love in poetry
and faith from essence.

56

A woman and her cow and donkey
and a couple of white sheep
lay on grassland moist in their blood as hips of meat.
Over them birds of prey hover,
then land and slowly reap
in wonder how abundant nature's table is
with so much to eat.

They were hungry, couldn't find anything for so many days
and, look, now there is plenty and further thence even more.
O, happy beast of prey that hunts,
robs at free will and slays,
takes what it needs,
does what it fancies and pays no score.

Woman and her household
lay down by oblivion forever hind.
Their blood stains grass and air
and sunset's leaden sky.
What they lent from faithful soil,
now they repay in kind with warning:
Last judgement has resolved verdict to apply.

57

I am here! Not there – where you now are.
And here is peace at the moment, maybe longer
But there is peril – walk of death without bar,
smoke, fire, thunders of thunder louder and stronger.

Tumultuous day passed after day without night and dawn,
sleepless hours of no time in rhythm of busy clock.
Over the river Styx souls are ferried by tireless Charon
who never stops being dependent as headman of his
stock.

And I am here safe and sound, but you are there –
in Hell, I suppose . For the Hell cannot be else or other.
Couldn't you provide anything better than WAR,
good Sir?
A WAR!
Born in sweat and blood like a baby from its mother.

58

The swallow, a little swift bird has flown again back.
Under my roof her mortar - nest is full of joy.
There she enters, turns within, extending her tiny neck,
peering out as from balcony resembling a mere toy.

Ocean going ship has master, crew and agent to meet.
Airplane got a thousand buttons to set on navigable chips.
Traveller takes counsel with map to find country,
city and street. Child has books to learn from learned
with spasm on his lips.

My little swallow has none. All is written in her chest
while still in egg which bursting lifts the mist to be
aware.
Earth is her mother, teacher and science
that lead her to nest
across the oceans and many lands
to enjoy life happy and fair.

59

Snow is snowing and cold rain
spreads colder sludge.
Cold wind plucks weathered heights
and its shrubby deck.
Words must be unspoken
not to prevent tell-tales and grudge
but to spare the breath to warm hearts that warmth lack.

Faithful soldiers keep guard
although the tempest keeps treating.
Damp and frozen they await
the enemy's scouts or charge
They wonder where is due launcher's missile
after flashing
for they count, waiting with silent smiles
when it misses their dug in marge.

How can I stand idle
knowing that they shiver out of grace
defending us on and HOME
that with LAND carries sacred mark?
I am calling out from this mount of pain
to the conscience of the human race:
"Let's tear off the amnion of punishment
bestowed upon us by Noah's ark."

60

When beaver starts to build the house
he has a lot to hike
in order to provide logs and timber
for tunnels trail to obscure.
And the bees passionate and clever,
work happily never in strike.
Free creatures as busy bees hurry
to prepare a shelter that's secure.

So does the family of man, dreaming
about a warm home to rest,
to abide and spend too dear a time
allotted to them.
Stout-hearted men dedicate
their whole life doing their best,
for house and home mean a sacred place,
shrine of living stem.

And when dreams came true
and desire fulfilment got
then the reverse impetus
overwhelms the accomplished deed
and destroys all.
Bloody mercenaries, *Sans-çu-lotte*
repeat misdeeds out of mind
while bee and beaver mind the need.

61

A man and his horse worked together
as lord and slave:
The better the horse hauled,
the more hiding he got from the lord,
just to refresh his fickle mood
which evil tempers crave
thus inflicting pain on purpose –
more by act than with word.

One day the horse couldn't stand
the humiliation, neighed with dart,
went wild, reared and pulled over a stony wall
the wagon and wagoner
littering around parts of the structure
that was its damned cart
and in non plus stopped,
trembled continuing to whinny and rear.

The man astounded stood in awe,
set and thought of his fault:
why was he a devil to faithful animal
that earned his bread?
Then he turned to talk genially as if he sang:
"You are my salt."
Hour after hour he kept talking
from afar being shaken and sad.

Lastly the horse surrendered
and let the man seize its neck again
awaiting poor end as one that knew
only scourge and toil,
But the man embraced it,
petted and kissed its neck and loosed rein,
then they went side by side with tight feelings
as the seed in rich soil.

62

Talk, talk to me O human highness with thrilling voice!
Speak willing and let me pronounce whatever talk.
Loose your tongue stream in the wind of choice
as flying birds and mute fish or ox under yoke.

Talk about Trojan horse, Sodom and Gomorra,
wretched Crusade,
repeat the story of burned Rome,
Termopili and Berlin in flame.
Keep talking about Stalingrad,
Sutjeska, Vukovar as death made
Hiroshima, and revolutions that eat human flesh
without claim.

Coo then as dove, coo at evening and at flushing daybreak!
Speak slow and calm like water after roaring falls at
pause!
Speak quick as a rolling avalanche for runaways sake!
Speak to ease our burden, resound through accord of
better cause.

Greet man and woman, baby and playful child on way.
Speak to grass, milk before drink and gentle, horned cow,
to rain, fruitful fields, rainbow and poppies in May
for the din of our voices transmits
the code of life from ever to now.

63

Long is the way to knowledge
affected by disappointment and retrace.
One learns from past written in heavy books
with tons of pages,
the others from inspirations that simmer
through roots of race,
and third neither search nor ask, relying on daily wages.

They elaborate every event and as actors on stage play
"How?" and "Why?"
Then watch and laugh happily, sitting in the middle
of the circus, enjoying a high esteem,
while we walk crucified over blood and tears,
compelled to die
without witness and judge or lecture
able to enlighten our dream.

You have seen at last what was hidden in depth
of time behind us
and what it meant: "Antemurale Christianitatis"
made of hearts like China Wall.
Thus we stood on frontier of rough historic
sea for you to pass
and no one ever shouted
"Ave Croatia, Mother of Liberty, thank you for all!"

64

Happy are the people that didn't experience
migration's waves!
They never dream about flood,
fire and guns or launchers' rattle.
And happy are migrants that far from their country
suffer not as slaves
but yearn after their homeland
as eagle after height or hawk after battle.

Now behold, they leave their home and all
acquired and got in heritage:
expecting mothers, little ones and old with
Two World Wars on their backs.
They are passing by the unscrupulous world
as by a forlorn hermitage
carrying conscience of human race as rotten potatoes
in worn out sacks.

Over Balcan, chained by chains of time refugees
flee to West from East.
Flee or are driven to bondage and slavery
in the lawless environs
where they melt as snow,
expiring as ferments in forgotten yeast,
and the rust of civilisation overruns the event
settling in faith as in a nest of iron.

65

The waves rush and charge on rocks along the sea bank,
splash the gravel and menace beneath my seating stone.
I gaze and survey its vast labour in tireless rank
that moves outside as feeble flesh sustained by inner
bone.

The waves come from afar and roll from somewhere
to anywhere;
always the same and likewise different murmur and roar,
The things come and go but waves persist to
wave and adhere
to principles of movement that first dissipate
and then restore.

The endless creative powers roll on and build the fear,
The vast liquid ocean coolly embraces boiling metallic
ore,
hisses here and there, keeps vigil in order to steer
the revival of secret cause repeating, "More and more!"

66

"Timeo Danaos et dona ferentes" Virgil, poet and sage,
forced Aeneas to convey an ancient event into lasting
rule,
Since we are like waves that work repeating
in order to engage
in continuous movement: first to warm
and multiply then select and cool.

You greet and shake hands and smile as friends for ever
and then knife the back and step on human seed
as on snake,
Thus we cannot discern good from bad and no endeavour
can compensate for the horror executed
at threshold of wake.

Listen then to what Aeneas said if the truth
may win your wicked lust.
Don't dissemble a superb bard you grey cur
chained to promise,
Don't stray through wood as wolf
bleeding to death in gust
for there isn't anyone to dress your wound,
nor your sordid lips to kiss.

67

It's great to be alive, to awake
with morning sun and be whole,
to hold life by head instead of
by tail and jubilate:
"Glory, glory hallelujah!":
playing once more a blessed role
on stage of presence performing
miracles so as to create.

I look and see a thousand eyes
all looking for something to see,
and participate, in search
for congruent physical mean where to sink.
As a ship on voyage going over the ocean
only to moor under the lee,
So do these eyes overstrained to behold,
marvel and then blink.

It's very sad to look at a worm
during metamorphoses in pain.
How can we survive with as much pain
and bleeding tears
that soak the native soil in succession
as autumnal rain?
Indeed, it's great to be alive
although stuck in disaster dying for cheers.

68

You are educated to preach and incite movement of change,
push and pull like whirlwind and draw to explode
unaware people charged by hate and revenge
sending them to trot like hunted fox down its sobbing road.

Tease the crowd like animal to exert its burden of anger.
Lead them over trackless mount to calm of cheating sound
that stumble, ramble, ramp as furious ram and stagger
writing vain history by bleeding feet on frozen ground.

But your spirit swagger as banner flutter and instigate
soliciting pride to take on oath at shrine of sacrificed men.
Over the vast space we are doomed to navigate
our damned vessel sideways of
"Omen" at long last "Amen."

69

The other day I crushed an ant by chance and left stays.
His kin's ant passed, sniffed at and started to run.
At first up and down, then returned to one that lays
and again ran around looking from where the danger
spun.

Then he took his brother and carried it step by step,
then down and again up persisting hard hurdle to cross.
No man would ever do the same standing at the gap
with his dead comrade thoroughly indulged in common
loss.

O ant, ant! O little busy creature in selfish wood.
You are the giant of pure spiritual sample.
Your little heart stands aloft as Himalayan hood.
Show us the bond of your pledge and your temple.

ANNEX

I

A woman ran away from shooting and killing raid
as war is flaming through a country where human plague
overtakes the command of life and its rise and fade,
leaving the existence to hang on sheer luck,
absurd as vague.

She shoulders her little boy,
fatally wounded in sudden strife,
and hurries up observing in shudder apparitions dark.
"Mother!" said the boy
"Leave me alone and save your life!"
But she tore through the air
as through sea does an unpredictable shark.

"Mother!" said he again
"Run away since you can and let me die."
But she clinched him tighter and quicken by funny gegs.
After a while she stopped,
lowered him to rock beside Lorelei –
stone-still, cold in cold, then flew off as bird without
legs.

II

She stood down headed looking nowhere as empty well
in which waste should be thrown and hid.
She stood as one that has nowhere to dwell.
As a book of truth that nobody wished to read.

"Tell me" said the father "my only one, what they did?"
And she looked at him as in sun without light –
a dark ball that hangs above waters under leaden lid,
then again lowered her head to avoid father's sight.

She hears within men's boast and ironic groan in grip.
Did you bull in the bitch? No! I broke her right through!
And animals never rape their immature kind
nor tear them and rip.
She grieved painfully for out of her horrid state
new being ventured to brew.

III

"Mother, I overhear something behind
like sobbing, crawling. Is it wolf or deer?"
"Be calm my son, the night is blind
and we cannot guess what we hear."

"Mother, can't we stop for a short sleep?"
"Oh, be quiet, don't talk till we get clear."
And they run and run and sometimes creep
and dash on in manner hopeless and queer.

Then the fir quivered – "Woe is me!" uttered Mother,
falling down as shot fox in fowl – run.
And the boy tried to lift her struck dumb, rather.
Then lay beside her in warm blood as in womb re-done.

IV

"Rise up my brother, rise up! It's war!"
"Oh, is it again by Jove, again you say?
Why did I die then and give my life?
Remember how they killed me in a terrible way?"

"It's war my brother can't you get up at all?
Save us once more, help us to survive, please!"
And he rose from time as from ocean an atoll,
forced the dream out and resurrection set at ease.

Then all people of the Earth got up and rushed like a
stream
to meet Messiah, after age of turmoil and futile
endeavour.
Awake! Awake! Here is the question of our unaware
dream.
The last minute of suffering is striking.
Awake then, now or never.